PARTY TIME!

PLAN A SLEEPOVER PARTY

STEPHANIE WATSON

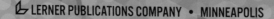
LERNER PUBLICATIONS COMPANY • MINNEAPOLIS

To my son, Jake.
You're always the life of any party.

Lerner Publications Company
A division of Lerner Publishing Group, Inc.
241 First Avenue North
Minneapolis, MN 55401 USA

For reading levels and more information, look up this title at
www.lernerbooks.com.

Main text set in Gill Sans MT Std 11/14.
Typeface provided by Monotype Typography.

Library of Congress Cataloging-in-Publication Data

Watson, Stephanie, 1969–
        Plan a sleepover party / by Stephanie Watson.
             p.   cm.
        Includes index.
        ISBN 978–1–4677–3832–3 (lib. bdg. : alk. paper)
        ISBN 978–1–4677–4724–0 (eBook)
        1. Sleepovers—Juvenile literature. 2. Children's parties—Juvenile
    literature. I. Title.
    GV1205.W3796 2015
    793.2'1—dc23   2013037669

Manufactured in the United States of America
1 – PC – 7/15/14

TABLE OF CONTENTS

WHY HOST A SLEEPOVER PARTY?

WHAT'S YOUR IDEA OF THE PERFECT PARTY? Hanging out with your friends all night? Watching scary movies and telling ghost stories until everyone screams? Pigging out on hot fudge sundaes and homemade cookies straight out of the oven? Staying up *waaay* past your bedtime, then curling up in your sleeping bag and snoozing until lunchtime the next day? Then a sleepover is the perfect party for you!

So what if it's not your birthday? You don't need a special reason to throw a slumber party. All you need are a few friends, some yummy snacks, and a few cool game ideas. Even if you've never hosted a party in your life, you can still throw a sleepover so amazing that your friends will be talking about it for years to come.

This book will teach you all the tips and tricks for hosting the ultimate slumber party. Not sure whom to invite? You'll learn how to build your dream guest list—without hurting anyone's feelings. Can't decide whether to make smoothies or sundaes? We've got your menu covered. You'll even learn how to feed your pickiest friends!

Read on to get the scoop on planning, hosting, and recovering from your next sleepover. Soon you'll be such a slumber party expert that *all* your friends will be coming to you for party-planning advice!

CHAPTER ONE

PREP FOR YOUR PARTY

FIRST THINGS FIRST—you can't host a party without a parent's okay. So how do you broach the subject?

broach = to introduce a subject

If a big occasion is coming up, you've got the perfect excuse. You can say, "Guess what kind of birthday (or graduation or whatever) party I want to have?" Or come up with another good reason to throw a party. Maybe you could ask your family if they'd reward you for something good, like:

⟹ Getting straight As for a month

⟹ Cleaning your room every day for a month

⟹ Finishing the school year

⟹ Collecting money for an important cause, such as a local animal shelter or a children's hospital

Or see if a parent is game for striking up a deal with you. In this scenario, you ask a parent to come up with something he or she would like you to do. Once you've done whatever it is your parent requests, you get your party!

Want to host a party? Talk to your parents first.

GIRLS (OR BOYS) ONLY?

Should you have a coed slumber party? Usually it's best to invite only girls if you're a girl and only boys if you're a boy. But that's up to you—and your family. If you do make your party coed, make sure you have an adult chaperone. And consider splitting up the girls and boys for sleeping.

coed = including both boys and girls

chaperone = an adult who attends a social event to provide supervision

PICK A THEME

Picking a party theme is easy. All you need is a little imagination.

What are your FAVORITE THINGS to do?

☆ Love music? Host a DJ party! Hang some lights, spin your favorite tunes, and dance all night!

☆ Into movies? Turn your home into a theater. Pop some popcorn and put your favorite flicks on the screen.

Party tip: Individual popcorn boxes make your home feel even more like a theater.

luau = a Hawaiian-style party. Luaus often include grass skirts, flowered necklaces called leis, and hula dancing.

☆ Can't get enough of the beach? Have a luau! Make your own beach with some plastic palm trees and beach chairs. Hand out towels, leis, and grass skirts. Put on some ukulele tunes or ocean sound effects, and pretend you and your friends are relaxing in the sun and surf!

☆ Are you a sports fanatic? Ask your friends to wear the local team's colors—and paint your faces to match! Serve hot dogs, pretzels, and other game-time snacks. Turn on the big game, and cheer on the home team!

We've got even more slumber party themes at the end of this book. But don't stop with our ideas. You can throw just about any kind of party you can dream up.

YOUR TO-DO LIST

When planning your perfect slumber party, use a planner or a calendar on a phone to remind you of these dates.

FOUR WEEKS TO GO

- ❑ Ask a parent for permission.
- ❑ Pick out invites.
- ❑ Write a guest list.
- ❑ Choose a party theme.

THREE WEEKS TO GO

- ❑ Send out invites.
- ❑ Plan the menu.
- ❑ Buy or make decorations.

TWO WEEKS TO GO

- ❑ Make sure your friends have RSVP'd (that means they said yes or no).
- ❑ Get the entertainment ready—pick music and movies.

ONE WEEK TO GO

- ❑ Hang decorations.
- ❑ Buy food (with a parent's help).
- ❑ Fill the goody bags, if you'll be handing any out.

ONE DAY TO GO

- ❑ Pick out your outfit.
- ❑ Prep the food.
- ❑ Run through the party schedule with a parent or a friend.
- ❑ Get ready to party!

Plan a party budget with a parent before you shop so there are no arguments at the store.

Party tip: To boost the attendance and the fun, be sure to consider the date of your party carefully.

PICK A DATE

When should you have your slumber party? This step takes a little bit of thought.

First, pick a night when you don't have to get up early for school the next day. There's nothing more boring than a slumber party with an early bedtime. A weekend or a school holiday is best for staying up late.

Avoid schedule conflicts. Don't plan your party the night before the big soccer game if all your friends are on the team. Also avoid traditionally busy times of the year—like Thanksgiving weekend. And definitely don't plan your party on another friend's birthday. You don't want to compete for guests—or steal your friend's thunder on his or her special day.

Come up with a few possible dates. Then ask your friends if they're free. Schedule your party on the day that works for most of your friends.

GET A PARENT INVOLVED

Parents can be a big help as you plan your party. There are some things you just can't do without them—like shopping for groceries and decorations.

At the same time, you want the freedom to design your party your way. So talk to your mom or dad ahead of time. Tell your parent what you'll need help with and what you want to do on your own. Just make sure your mom or dad is cool with everything you're doing so you don't get in trouble later.

YOUR GUEST LIST

With slumber parties, smaller really is better. You don't want to invite your whole class and have them take over—or, worse, trash your house. So decide on a number. How many people will comfortably fit in your living room or basement without it being too crowded? Four? Six? Ten? Got a number? Good—now you can move on to making your list.

Whom should you invite? You can't include everyone, but you don't want to hurt anybody's feelings either.

Start with your BFFs—your two or three closest friends. Then step outside your inner circle. Are there any cool kids you like hanging out with at school? Finally, add some new kids to the mix. Think about friends you know from outside of school—from summer camp or your sports team, for instance.

Party tip: You might want to invite friends with common interests to your party. If most of your guests love musicals or sports, it won't matter if they come from different schools or towns!

NO-DRAMA PARTIES

Unless you want your party taken over by bickering, choose your guests wisely. Don't invite Samantha *and* Jen if you know they're in a huge fight. Also, don't invite the class gossip who'll tell everyone at school all the details about your party on Monday. Save the drama for another time.

INVITES

Now that you've got your party theme and date nailed down, you need to send out the invites. You have some different options here. One way to go is to buy invitations at a store. They'll cost a few dollars, but all the work is done for you.

Don't want to spend the money on paper invites? You can send them online with the help of a website like Evite. Ask your mom or dad to help you design them.

Once you have your invites chosen, fill in all the details about your party. There are five pieces of information you need to include.

Ask your mom or dad to help you create invitations online. You will need your friends' e-mail addresses.

SAMPLE INVITE

What: The type of party

When: The date and time of the party

Where: The address

Special info: What do you want your guests to wear? Is there anything special you want them to bring?

RSVP: This is short for *"répondez s'il vous plaît."* That's a fancy French way of saying, "Are you coming to my party or not?" Include your phone number here so your friends can "répondez" (reply), if you sent out paper invites. If you went with online invites, your guests will probably just need to click a button to tell you if they're coming.

You're Invited to
Missy's Fashion Makeover
Sleepover!

When: Friday, August 1, 8 p.m.

Where: My house! 1234 Small Town Lane, Doe Ridge, TN 22222

What to bring: Your sleeping bag, pillow, pajamas, makeup, and some favorite jewelry!

RSVP: Missy—555-123-4567

Here's an example of how your party invite might look.

Be careful about when you pass out invites. DON'T do it in the middle of school. And especially don't hand Julie her invitation right in front of Lisa, whom you're not inviting. You'll only hurt Lisa's feelings. One surefire way to avoid hurt feelings is to mail invitations to your friends' homes. Evites are another good option for avoiding hurt feelings.

Party tip:
If you have to deliver your invites in person, do it after school so you don't hurt anyone's feelings.

bling = something sparkly, such as glitter or jewelry

MAKE YOUR OWN INVITES

You can show off your creative flair by making your own party invitations. Start with some colored construction paper. Cut it into fun shapes. For example, if you're having a pizza party, cut your invites into pie-shaped circles. Then glue on cutout paper "toppings." If it's a makeup party, put lipstick "kisses" all over the paper.

Write the details about your party in marker. Then add a little bling! Sprinkle on glitter, or add some colored stickers to get your friends' attention.

DECORATIONS

Party decorating can be as simple or as fancy as you like! It all depends on your time, budget, and imagination.

Here are a few ideas to make your home look festive:

⇨ Drape streamers or beads down open doorways to turn your place into a dance club.

⇨ Cut stars and moons out of shiny paper, and tape them to the ceiling to make a night sky.

⇨ Blow up balloons and write words on them in colored markers. *Party, dance,* and *sleepover* are good words to write on your balloons. Then scatter them around the room.

⇨ Make a hangout space filled with pillows, sleeping bags, and beanbag chairs where you and your friends can chill.

⇨ Set up tents in your living room or basement to make an indoor campsite.

Party tip: You can go online or to a library to find directions for making no-sew pillowcases to add color to your room.

PLAN YOUR MENU

The best sleepover party menu is full of finger foods. They're fun and easy to eat. Gooey treats and fried snacks are fine to include, but try throwing in some healthful fruits and veggies too. Variety is good, and it's smart to have some better-for-you options.

Remember to ask all your guests if they have allergies—such as to peanuts or milk. Nothing will ruin a party faster than having to take one of your friends to the hospital!

If you've got friends who are picky eaters, vary the menu. Include a lot of different foods so there's something everyone will like.

Create the menu with a parent. Your parent can supervise the cooking too.

Here are a few ideas for your menu:

☆ Veggies and hummus dip
☆ Grilled chicken and veggie kebobs
☆ Pigs in a blanket
☆ Whole wheat crackers with mozzarella cheese

☆ Mini-bagel pizzas
☆ Chicken or beef sliders
☆ Chocolate chip cookies
☆ Berries dipped in chocolate

SLUMBER-PARTY RECIPE: MICROWAVE S'MORES

Who said you need a campfire to make s'mores? You can cook them in the microwave in less than thirty seconds!

INGREDIENTS:
1 square chocolate
1 marshmallow
2 graham cracker squares

DIRECTIONS:
1. Place the chocolate square and the marshmallow on one graham cracker square.
2. Place it on a paper towel in the microwave.
3. Cook for 15 seconds, or until the marshmallow gets puffy.
4. Cover with the other graham cracker square.
5. Eat your tasty treat!

CHAPTER TWO

THE PARTY'S ON!

YOU'VE BEEN PLANNING AND PREPPING FOR WEEKS. Finally, it's almost time for your party. About an hour before your guests arrive, make sure your home is ready.

✓ Are the decorations hung?

✓ Is the food ready?

✓ Are the music and movies good to go?

✓ Are the games set up?

If you answered yes to all of these questions, you're ready for the party to start!

GREETING YOUR GUESTS

When your guests arrive, be at the door to meet them. Smile and be polite!

You might say: "Hi, Aisha. Welcome to my party! I'm so glad you could come!"

If your guests haven't been to your place before, give them a tour. Introduce people who don't know one another. A good intro might be to say: "Olivia, this is Ava. She's on my soccer team. Ava, Olivia is in my class at school." Also introduce your friends to your family members.

Then give your friends a preview of what you'll be doing that night. For example: "We're going to make our own pizzas first. Then later, we'll play some games, do karaoke, and watch a movie."

karaoke = a type of entertainment where people sing into a microphone to recorded music

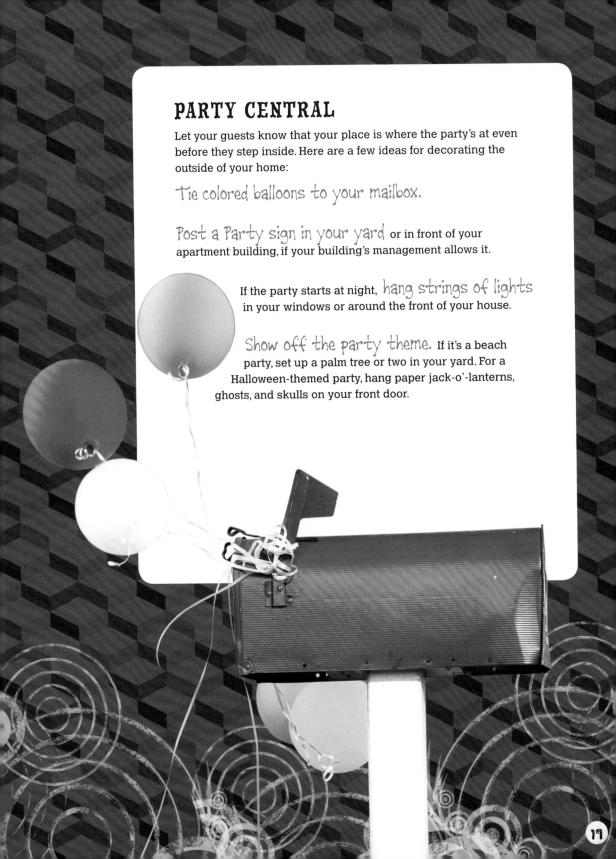

PARTY CENTRAL

Let your guests know that your place is where the party's at even before they step inside. Here are a few ideas for decorating the outside of your home:

Tie colored balloons to your mailbox.

Post a Party sign in your yard or in front of your apartment building, if your building's management allows it.

If the party starts at night, hang strings of lights in your windows or around the front of your house.

Show off the party theme. If it's a beach party, set up a palm tree or two in your yard. For a Halloween-themed party, hang paper jack-o'-lanterns, ghosts, and skulls on your front door.

PARTY PICS

Every awesome party needs some paparazzi, and yours is no exception! Get a parent to take pictures of all the fun. Then you can make mini-scrapbooks—a cool gift for your guests!

Just be careful about sharing photos online. Remember that you can't always control who sees your pics on Facebook, Instagram, and other social media sites. So don't post any pictures you wouldn't want to get out. That includes pics of your friends in their pj's. They'll never forgive you!

paparazzi = photographers who snap pictures of celebrities and sell them to magazines

 Party tip: Take turns taking pics so everyone is shown having fun. Have a friend who is camera shy? Appoint him or her to be the "official photographer" for the night!

18

PARTY FLOW

You want every minute of your party to be as fun as it can be for you and your friends. To make sure the night turns out to be extra special, plan it out from start to finish.

Your schedule could look something like this:

★ 6 p.m.—guests arrive

★ 7 p.m.—pizza and ice cream

★ 8 p.m.—dance contest

★ 9 p.m.—mani-pedis

★ 10 p.m.—scavenger hunt

★ 10:30 p.m.—movie time!

★ 12 p.m.—ghost stories

★ 10 a.m.—pancake breakfast

Don't worry about staying on schedule if everyone is having fun!

If the night doesn't go exactly according to schedule, don't panic. Go with the flow! Don't switch off a movie your guests are enjoying just to get to the ghost stories. Part of being a great host is knowing when your guests are having fun and keeping the momentum going.

PARTY ACTIVITIES

Need some cool party activities? Here are a few fun ideas:

→ **MASTER CHEF.** Set out a few ingredients, like pizza or sugar cookies and toppings. Let your friends make their own culinary masterpieces (with an adult supervising, of course). Then pick the winner. A prize goes to the most delicious-looking creation.

→ **Murder Mystery.** Pretend one of your guests has met an untimely end. Give your guests some clues and let them figure out whodunit.

→ **Spa Night.** Ask a parent to hire a teenage neighbor, a family friend, or a relative to do mani-pedis and makeup for all your guests.

→ **Slumber Party Idol.** Have guests who are up for it sing along to their favorite song. Then the host picks a winner.

culinary = having to do with cooking, especially cooking good food

HOW TO BE THE PERFECT PARTY HOST

You're in charge of the party. That means it's up to you to make sure all your friends are having fun.

Don't let any of your friends feel left out. Make sure everyone gets a turn—whether it's at playing video games or having their nails done.

If one of your friends is sitting alone or looking left out, bring her into the activities. You could say, "Hey, Emma! We're about to do charades, and you're so good at it." Or "Sophia, didn't you say you've seen this movie, like, twenty times? What's your favorite part?"

It's up to you to help all of your friends have fun together.

HOUSE RULES

You don't want your friends to run all over and trash your home—and neither do your parents! With a parent's help, set a few ground rules at the start of your party. Those rules should include the following:

» **Which rooms your friends can use and which are off-limits**

» **How loud you can crank the music**

» **What kinds of movies you can watch (G, PG)**

» **Where in the house you can't take food (for example, no food on the couch or in the living room)**

» **How late you can stay up**

WHEN TO GO TO SLEEP

No matter how much you love to stay up late and gossip, at some point, it will be time to curl up in your sleeping bags and say good night. Your mom or dad might set a bedtime. But even if there's no set bedtime, eventually everyone's eyelids will start to droop.

When it is time for lights out, respect your guests. Keep the room quiet so everyone can sleep. Turn off the music and TV. If you've got a few noisy friends who just won't quiet down, have a parent ask them to settle in for the night.

QUIET ZONE

Everyone's got his or her own sleepover party routine. Some kids want to talk until dawn. Others need a full eight hours of sleep or they get grumpy.

Set aside a quiet place for your friends who want to crash early. You could use an empty bedroom, den, or a tucked-away part of the basement. Sleepy friends can zonk out when they're ready, and the party can still go on!

AFTER THE PARTY

ONE OF THE BEST THINGS about a slumber party is that you don't have to say good-bye at the end of the night. The fun can go on well into the next morning!

If you partied past midnight, you may have a sleepy group. But once they get hungry enough, they'll crawl out of their sleeping bags to eat.

You'll need a parent's help cooking breakfast. Here are some easy foods that can feed a whole group of hungry kids:

☆ Scrambled eggs

☆ French toast

☆ Sausage or bacon

☆ Pancakes

☆ Fruit salad

Party tip: If you want your friends to wake up, make something that smells terrific—like cinnamon rolls. No one will be able to resist!

TOP-YOUR-OWN PANCAKES

For a fun and easy slumber party breakfast, make a do-it-yourself pancake bar. Ask a parent to cook a stack of flapjacks. Then put out bowls of toppings. These could include the following treats:

flapjacks = another word for pancakes

★ Fruit—strawberries, bananas, and blueberries

★ Nuts—walnuts, almonds, and pecans (just make sure your guests don't have any nut allergies!)

★ Syrups—maple, strawberry, and chocolate

★ Spreads—butter and jam

★ Sweet extras—chocolate chips, sprinkles, honey, and cinnamon

Then see who can make the most creative pancakes!

GOODY BAGS

You don't *have* to give out goody bags at your party. But if you want to leave your friends with some special party favors, here are some ideas:

⤷ *Spa bag.* Fill these bags with mini nail polish, hand cream, and a nail file.

⤷ SLEEPOVER BAG. Include a toothbrush, some toothpaste, a small hairbrush, a sleep mask, and star stickers.

⤷ SPORTS BAG. Stuff this one with baseball cards, a whistle, a toy car, and a basketball or football eraser.

⤷ ARTSY BAG. Put in some crayons, Magic Markers, and a small drawing notebook.

Once each bag is filled with favors, you can tie it with a piece of ribbon or some simple colored yarn to make it decorative.

Party tip: Even a plain brown bag is fun with some letters cut collage style and glued on. Try it with pictures too—glue on sport stars or fashion models from your favorite magazines.

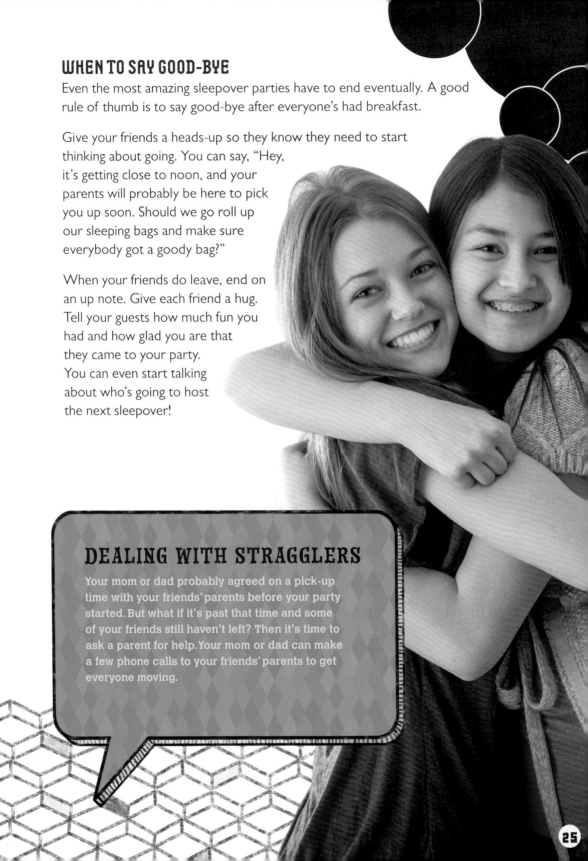

WHEN TO SAY GOOD-BYE

Even the most amazing sleepover parties have to end eventually. A good rule of thumb is to say good-bye after everyone's had breakfast.

Give your friends a heads-up so they know they need to start thinking about going. You can say, "Hey, it's getting close to noon, and your parents will probably be here to pick you up soon. Should we go roll up our sleeping bags and make sure everybody got a goody bag?"

When your friends do leave, end on an up note. Give each friend a hug. Tell your guests how much fun you had and how glad you are that they came to your party. You can even start talking about who's going to host the next sleepover!

DEALING WITH STRAGGLERS

Your mom or dad probably agreed on a pick-up time with your friends' parents before your party started. But what if it's past that time and some of your friends still haven't left? Then it's time to ask a parent for help. Your mom or dad can make a few phone calls to your friends' parents to get everyone moving.

MAKE YOUR OWN PARTY PHOTO ALBUM

One fun way to let your friends know you're happy they attended your party is to send them an album of party pictures.

WHAT YOU NEED:

- ❑ a printer
- ❑ pictures from your party
- ❑ photo paper
- ❑ tape or glue
- ❑ colored construction paper
- ❑ three-hole punch
- ❑ ribbon or yarn

WHAT YOU DO:

1. Print out pictures from the party on photo paper.

2. Tape or glue them to pieces of colored construction paper.

3. Punch holes down the left side of the paper.

4. Use ribbon or yarn to tie the pages into a book.

Party tip:
Use markers or paint pens to write sayings like "YOU GO, GIRL!" or "ROCK IT ALL NIGHT!" underneath your party photos.

Make your photo album even more fun by inviting your bestie to help go through the photos.

THE BIG CLEANUP

Even the most organized party can get messy. There are dishes to wash, decorations to take down, and sleeping bags to put away. But don't panic! Cleaning up doesn't have to be a pain. To make it less overwhelming, turn it into a game. Set a timer, and see how fast you can accomplish each task. For example, see if you can take down all the decorations and put them into storage in five or ten minutes. You can also play fun music while you work. That keeps the party feeling going even after your guests have gone home.

THANK-YOU NOTES

Even if it wasn't your birthday and you didn't get any gifts, sending thank-you notes or e-mails—or even a simple, friendly text—is a nice gesture. A thank-you message tells your friends you're glad they came to your party.

gesture = a way to show that you feel a particular way

Just like your invites, you can make thank-you notes yourself. Or you can buy them at the store if you'd prefer.

Once your thank-yous have been sent, you can start thinking about the next fun party you're going to throw!

Party tip: A thank-you message lets your guests know you appreciate having them as friends.

SLEEPOVER PARTY THEME IDEAS

Check out these awesome themes to inspire you next time you throw a slumber party!

OVERNIGHT GLAM THEME

Treat your friends to a night at the spa. Get a teenager in the neighborhood to do mani-pedis, facials, and makeup. Ask your mom or maybe an older sister or a cousin if you can borrow some of her dresses to get all glammed up. Or find some cool dresses, hats, and coats at your local thrift store. **PARTY FAVORS:** nail polish, lip gloss, and nail file.

CAMPOUT THEME

Who said you had to drive all the way out into the woods and fight off bears to go camping? Set up tents right in your backyard—or basement! Then tell ghost stories—just like at a real campout. **PARTY FAVORS:** flashlights with your friends' names on them.

CHEFS' NIGHT THEME

Let your friends cook their own dinner. It's more fun that way! Set out pizza dough and bowls of toppings. Or put out plates of plain pasta and let them add ingredients from vegetables to cheese to meatballs.

SPORTS FANS THEME

Bring the sports stadium to your home! Pick your favorite sport—football, baseball, racing, or hockey. Decorate your place with banners from your favorite team. Serve snack foods like nachos, hot dogs, and chicken fingers. Then watch the game on the big screen.

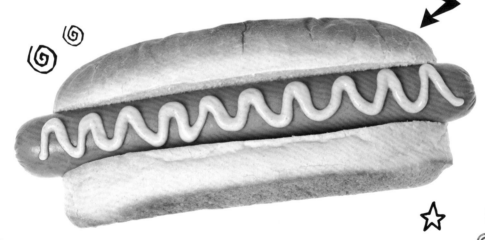

THE PERFECT SLEEPOVER PARTY PLAYLIST

Not sure which tunes to load onto your phone or music player for your party? Here are some hits that will have your guests dancing all night:

"Baby," Justin Bieber

"Call Me Maybe," Carly Rae Jepsen

"Get'cha Head in the Game," *High School Musical*

"Girls Just Want to Have Fun," Cyndi Lauper

"Hit the Lights," Selena Gomez

"I Gotta Feeling," Black Eyed Peas

"Party in the USA," Miley Cyrus

"Roar," Katy Perry

FURTHER INFORMATION

Braun, Eric. *Plan an Outdoor Party.* Minneapolis: Lerner Publications, 2015.
Want to throw a cool backyard party? This book includes all the tips you'll need to get started.

Family Education
http://fun.familyeducation.com/sleepover-party-planner/63053.html
This site has party planning info for both kids and parents.

Hands-On Crafts for Kids. *Perfect Kids' Parties: 12 Fantastic Theme Celebrations.* New York: Sterling, 2006.
Stumped on a party theme idea? This book has a dozen of them, from a carnival party to an outer space blast.

Kara's Party Ideas
http://www.karaspartyideas.com
Party planner Kara Allen shares her secrets to hosting a party your friends will never forget.

Kenney, Karen Latchana. *Cool Slumber Parties: Perfect Party Planning for Kids.* Minneapolis: Abdo, 2012.
Check out this book for more tips to help you plan your perfect sleepover party.

Lundsten, Apryl. *A Smart Girl's Guide to Parties.* Middleton, WI: American Girl, 2010.
Whether you're throwing a party or just going to one, this book will teach you everything you need to know to have a great time.

Spoonful
http://spoonful.com/parties
Get all your party planning tips in one place! Spoonful has ideas for recipes, decorations, and party games.

INDEX

PHOTO ACKNOWLEDGMENTS

The images in this book are used with the permission of: backgrounds © iStockphoto.com/Nenochka (geometric pattern) and © iStockphoto.com/IntergalacticDesignStudio (rolled ink frame); © Africa Studio/Shutterstock.com, p. 1; © JupiterImages/Thinkstock, pp. 4, 18 (bottom), 19; © iStockphoto.com/Kail Nine LLC, pp. 5, 7; © JupiterImages/Getty Images/Thinkstock, p. 6; © Jade/Blend Images/Getty Images, p. 8; © Andresr/Shutterstock.com, p. 9; © Yellow Dog Productions/Iconica/Getty Images, p. 10; © Monkey Business Images/The Agency Collection/Getty Images, p. 11 (top); © Stephen Simpson/The Image Bank/Getty Images, p. 11 (bottom); © iStockphoto.com/Kilukilu, pp. 12–13 (background); © BooHoo/Shutterstock.com, p. 12 (pajamas); © Chris Ryan/OJO Images/Getty Images, p. 13; © Alena Ozerova/Dreamstime.com, p. 14; © iStockphoto.com/Saturated, p. 15; © Victoria Snowber/Digital Vision/Getty Images, p. 17; © Reggie Casagrande/Photolibrary/Getty Images, p. 18 (top); © JupiterImages/Stockbyte/Getty Images, p. 20; © Garry Wade/The Image Bank/Getty Images, p. 21; © Prudkov/Shutterstock.com, p. 22; © Floortje/Vetta/Getty Images, p. 23; © iStockphoto.com/Taylor Hinton, p. 24; © John Fedele/Blend Images/Vetta/Getty Images, p. 25; © iStockphoto.com/btrenkel, p. 26; © Chris Howes/Wild Places Photography/Alamy, p. 27 (top); © Kidstock/Blend Images/Getty Images, p. 27 (bottom); © Gresel/Shutterstock.com, p. 28 (top); © iStockphoto.com/Dosecreative, p. 28 (bottom); © Lucie Lang/Shutterstock.com, p. 29 (top); © iStockphoto.com/Maceofoto, p. 29 (bottom).

Front cover: © iStockphoto.com/belchonock